EVERYTHING SUCKS

INTERIOR AND COVER DESIGNER: Tina Besa
ART PRODUCER: Sue Bischofberger
EDITOR: Morgan Shanahan
PRODUCTION MANAGER: Holly Haydash
PRODUCTION EDITOR: Melissa Edeburn

Illustrations © Creative Market, © DesignCuts, and © Shutterstock
Author Photo: Courtesy Danny Offer

ISBN: Print 978-1-64152-899-3

EVERYTHING

SUCKS

A

GRATITUDE JOURNAL

For People Who Have
Been Through Some Sh*t

TIFFANY REESE

ROCKRIDGE
PRESS

Gratitude unlocks the fullness of life. It turns what we have into enough, and more. It turns denial into acceptance, chaos to order, confusion to clarity. It can turn a meal into a feast, a house into a home, a stranger into a friend.

—MELODY BEATTIE,
AUTHOR

THIS BADASS JOURNAL
BELONGS TO

WHO'S READY TO GET THANKFUL UP IN HERE?!

So, you bought a gratitude journal called *Everything Sucks*, huh? We'll touch on that in a minute. First, gratitude. Here's my top 10 list:

+ my husband
+ my three kids
+ family
+ friends
+ free refills
+ music
+ murder podcasts
+ coffee
+ no line at the grocery store
+ three green lights in a row
+ coffee, again
+ the beach
+ social justice
+ plants
+ See's Candies
+ interspecies animal friendships
+ books
+ Netflix

Maybe you noticed my list of 10 was actually a list of 18. Sometimes the gratitude just flows—and I encourage you to let it do just that.

I first discovered the practice of gratitude—and all its benefits— as I struggled to combat childhood trauma, anxiety, and depression. I've struggled with my mental health for as long as I can remember. I was raised by alcoholic parents—both with personality disorders. I was told my entire life I wasn't enough. I wasn't thin, smart, quiet, pretty, or good enough. Surviving my childhood filled with emotional and physical abuse was difficult—but also all I knew. I graduated early and went to college at the age of 17 so I could distance myself from my family's chaos. Not long after, my parents divorced when my father went to prison. I felt incredibly isolated and was filled with resentment, and I also felt a deep desire to be loved.

At the age of 23 I became a parent myself and barely two years later my brother was murdered. My mental health hit an all-time low. The idea of "practicing gratitude" during a time of such pain and darkness almost sounds like a sick joke. But I realized I needed to focus on motherhood and let my love for my children and husband fuel my recovery. I knew I would never, ever allow my children to be exposed to the kinds of circumstances, environments, and ideas I was exposed to as a child. I knew I had to take care of myself if I was going to take care of them. I sought help. I joined support groups. I talked to professionals. I started establishing boundaries with others and began to let go of codependency. I started taking medication to help my depression and began treating my mind and body better.

As I began to value myself more, I started to understand that my childhood didn't need to dictate my adulthood. After choosing to become estranged from my family, I was, ironically, able to appreciate them more. I discovered it was okay to say goodbye to someone despite still loving them. I was able to accept them from a distance without missing them. I focused on the time I got to spend with my brother while he was alive instead of only thinking of my loss and grief.

I shifted my focus from "why me," "what if," and "WTF" to appreciating the growth that comes from challenge. Though my struggle with mental health and my biological family can sometimes make me feel powerless, thankfulness helps me remember who I am, what I'm capable of, and what's most important. It's like the world's most boring, but deeply healing, superpower.

This journal is for gratitude seekers who have walked through—or are currently struggling to survive—life's most challenging obstacles. Whereas the average gratitude journal has you choking on sunshine and butterflies, I wanted to create one that lets you feel free to be your genuine self—the one who curses and loses their temper, not the pretend one who eats Swiss chard and writes in weirdly earnest journals.

This book is dedicated to my husband and BFF, Michael, and our incredible children, Jude, Ruby, and Ozzy. I am forever in gratitude for the love, joy, and anxiety you bring into my life.

SO, WTF IS GRATITUDE AND HOW WILL THIS JOURNAL HELP ME FIND IT?

Gratitude is the quality of being thankful—of readiness to show appreciation for and to return kindness. Cultivating gratitude has been scientifically linked to higher life satisfaction and greater happiness. Research has also shown that keeping a gratitude journal can significantly increase your mental health and satisfaction, even if your life feels like a truly sucktastic hellscape. Those who regularly practice gratitude feel more positive overall, sleep better, express more compassion and kindness, have stronger immune systems, and probably act less like cranky jerks than those who don't. There is no downside to cultivating appreciation, unless you hate things like sleep and joy.

Okay, cool, you're into it. But what does gratitude practice look like in reality? It's shifting our focus from what went wrong to what went *right*. It's gently reminding ourselves that we once dreamed of where we are *now*. It's seeing the silver lining on a heaping pile of shit (improves soil quality!).

HOW TO USE THIS BOOK
(SPOILER ALERT: DO YOU, BOO)

This is a judgment-free journal—use it any way you please. You can even throw it across the room if you want to. Life is busy and the last thing you need is another thing to feel guilty about. Each prompt is intended for five minutes of reflection per day. However, you can also write in this journal less frequently. You're free to start on any page or skip around. Draw doodles of butts if it helps. There are no rules.

We're human, so we are going to have feelings other than gratitude when reflecting on hard shit. Good! This means you are allowing yourself to feel. Be honest with yourself and process what you need to before moving into thankfulness. It doesn't have to be pretty.

Anyone can seek gratitude no matter what their life looks like. I hope this journal will be a source of calm, growth, and joy—so you can take on whatever clusterfuck may come your way.

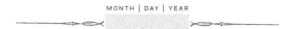

You may have seen the word "gratitude" so many times by now it's lost all meaning. What does gratitude mean to you?

We're a nation hungry for more joy: Because we're starving from a lack of gratitude.

—BRENÉ BROWN, RESEARCH PROFESSOR, AUTHOR, STORYTELLER

How do you define self-care? What are your three
favorite ways to show yourself extra love?

What makes you unique and why is that so fucking awesome?

Cherish forever what
makes you unique,
'cuz you're really a
yawn if it goes.

—BETTE MIDLER,
SINGER-SONGWRITER

Who makes you feel listened to and emotionally cared for that you don't pay to do so?

....

....

....

....

....

....

....

....

....

....

....

....

....

....

....

....

....

....

We learned about gratitude and humility—that so many people had a hand in our success, from the teachers who inspired us to the janitors who kept our school clean ... and we were taught to value everyone's contribution and treat everyone with respect.

—MICHELLE OBAMA,
LAWYER AND FORMER FIRST LADY

What are five of your favorite (legal) things to do to relax?

I'm so thankful
for that struggling
period. That time
is really great
where you have no
idea what's going
to happen.

—ABBI JACOBSON, COMEDIAN

Aside from farting and sex, what does your body help you do that you are most grateful for?

What childhood memories are you most thankful for?

Make choices that bring love and joy to your body. It's not about perfection; it's about love and gratitude for an amazing body that works hard and deserves your respect.

—ALYSIA REINER,
ACTOR

Who in your life is killing the gratitude game? How do they inspire you to improve yourself?

What are you thankful to know about yourself now that you didn't know a year ago?

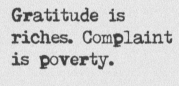

Gratitude is
riches. Complaint
is poverty.

—DORIS DAY,
ACTOR AND ACTIVIST

Aside from impeccable taste in gratitude journals,
what is your best personality trait?

I'm thankful I grew up the way I did. It made me a hard worker and insightful to other people's lives.

—RACHEL ROY,
FASHION DESIGNER

What are you doing today to be kinder to your body than you were doing a year ago? How are you showing your body you care and don't just think of it as a skin bag full of bones?

I finally realized that being grateful to my body was key to giving more love to myself.

—OPRAH WINFREY,
AMERICAN MEDIA EXECUTIVE

If you were to create a soundtrack of the songs that changed your life, what songs would you include? No music snobs will ever see this.

Who thinks you're beautiful — even when you look like a hot mess?

The more one does and sees and feels, the more one is able to do, and the more genuine may be one's appreciation of fundamental things like home, and love, and understanding companionship.

—AMELIA EARHART, AVIATOR

MONTH | DAY | YEAR

What are three horrible tasks you should stop bitching about because, honestly, you're lucky to have them to worry about?

We have to fill our
hearts with gratitude.
Gratitude makes
everything that we
have more than enough.

—SUSAN L. TAYLOR,
EDITOR AND JOURNALIST

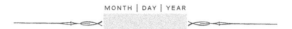

Who is your bestie and how do they improve your life? What do they understand about you that no one else does?

We are all more
blind to what
we have than to
what we have not.

—AUDRE LORDE, POET

What are your greatest talents or skills?
(I promise this isn't a job interview.)

Even though they probably screwed up big time, who do you need to forgive? Are you ready to do so? What positive lessons did you learn from this relationship?

What is it you're afraid of but could learn to
appreciate more? (Except spiders. Barf.)

"Thank you" is
the best prayer
that anyone could
say. I say that
one a lot. Thank you
expresses extreme
gratitude, humility,
understanding.

—ALICE WALKER, POET

What makes you feel like Beyoncé?

By cultivating gratitude
you eventually expand your
internal sense of what
is possible, regardless
of seeming obstacles and
challenges you go through.

—VERONICA SMITH, AUTHOR

As you sit here today, what problem do you most appreciate?
(This is an okay time to throw this journal across the room.)

True forgiveness is
when you can say,
"Thank you for that
experience."

—OPRAH WINFREY,
AMERICAN MEDIA
EXECUTIVE

What secret are you happy to keep?

Aside from the whole money thing, what do you like about your job?

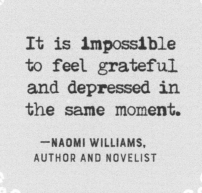

It is **impossible** to feel grateful and depressed in the same moment.

—NAOMI WILLIAMS,
AUTHOR AND NOVELIST

What shitty life experience was the hardest for you to grow through? How has that experience made you stronger?

. . . living in a
state of gratitude is
the gateway to grace.

—ARIANNA HUFFINGTON,
JOURNALIST

List five favorite things about your crib.

As a child, I didn't know
what I didn't have. I'm
thankful for the challenges
early on in my life because
now I have a perspective
on the world and . . . know
what's important.

—AMERICA FERRERA, ACTOR

What's your favorite #basic cheesy holiday or family tradition?

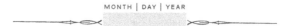

How can you show your family/chosen family more gratitude for their impact on your life (even when they are totally annoying)?

....

....

....

....

....

....

....

....

....

....

....

....

....

....

....

....

....

....

One can never pay
in gratitude: One
can only pay "in
kind" somewhere
else in life.

—ANNE MORROW LINDBERGH,
AUTHOR AND AVIATOR

What health care or medicine are you most appreciative for having access to?

Gratitude is
appreciation
for every moment
in your life—
a feeling of
abundance.

—BRENDA NATHAN, AUTHOR

Who makes you laugh until you pee a little bit?

We often take
for granted the
very things that
most deserve our
gratitude.

—CYNTHIA OZICK,
NOVELIST

Which bill are you most grateful to be able to afford to pay (this month, this year, in life)?

If you were to create a personal time capsule—and no one you know would ever see it—what would you put in it?

It's not happiness that
brings us gratitude.
It's gratitude that
brings us happiness.

—ANONYMOUS

What are the three most memorable compliments you've received?

When we focus on our gratitude, the tide of disappointment goes out and the tide of love rushes in.

—KRISTIN ARMSTRONG,
OLYMPIAN AND AUTHOR

What are three things you love about the way you look?

I want to thank my parents for raising me to have confidence that is somehow disproportionate with my looks and abilities. Well done. That is what all parents should do.

—TINA FEY,
ACTOR AND WRITER

Which technologies does your laziness appreciate most?

What has someone forgiven you for that you will never
forget (and probably won't tell anyone else)?

Gratitude is looking on the brighter side of life, even if it means hurting your eyes.

—ELLEN DEGENERES,
COMEDIAN

Besides chocolate, what can you be thankful
for, even on your darkest days?

I have noticed that
the Universe loves
Gratitude. The more
Grateful you are, the
more goodies you get.

—LOUISE HAY,
MOTIVATIONAL AUTHOR

If someone else were to describe your personality, what would they say? Would you agree?

So much has been given to me; I have not time to ponder over that which has been denied.

—HELEN KELLER,
AUTHOR AND ACTIVIST

Which of your five senses are you most grateful for? Why?

Which books are in your desert island library? What did
you learn about yourself through these stories?

My gratitude for good
writing is unbounded;
I'm grateful for it the
way I'm grateful for
the ocean.

—ANNE LAMOTT, AUTHOR

Of the places you've traveled, which are your three favorites?

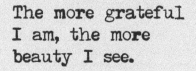

The more grateful
I am, the more
beauty I see.

—MARY DAVIS,
SPECIAL NEEDS ACTIVIST
AND CHIEF EXECUTIVE
OFFICER, SPECIAL OLYMPICS

When do you feel the safest and most cared for?

What about your personality do you find hard to embrace
or forgive? How has it been an asset in your life?

My socks may not
match, but my feet
are always warm.

—MAUREEN MCCULLOUGH,
ACTOR

How can you be less of a dick to Mother Earth? What
part of nature makes you feel completely Zen?

Life is precious,
and when you've
lost a lot of people,
you realize each
day is a gift.

—MERYL STREEP,
ACTOR

What is the best surprise you've ever had that didn't involve a pregnancy test?

When you focus on gratitude, positive things flow in more readily, making you even more grateful.

—LISSA RANKIN,
PHYSICIAN AND AUTHOR

Who inspires you to improve yourself without making you feel shame-y?

What's something you were once afraid to do
that was worth stressing TF out over?

My parents are the coolest of the cool on every single level, and it's because they have a deep appreciation for every moment of their lives.

—RASHIDA JONES, ACTOR

What was the highlight of your day? Your week? It
could be as simple as a really good sandwich.

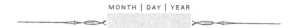

What is your favorite humblebrag?

Are you self-conscious about any part of your body?
How does this part of your body serve you in life?

Saying thanks to
the world, and
acknowledging your
own accomplishments,
is a great way
to feel good and
stay positive.

—RACHEL ROBINS, AUTHOR

What knowledge are you thankful for having that Google didn't teach you?

....

....

....

....

....

....

....

....

....

....

....

....

....

....

....

....

....

....

....

....

....

....

Name 10 First-World luxuries you take for granted. C'mon.
You've got 10. Do you have toilet paper in your house?

Be thankful for
what you have; you'll
end up having more.
If you concentrate on
what you don't have,
you will never, ever
have enough.

—OPRAH WINFREY,
AMERICAN MEDIA EXECUTIVE

What are some new (healthy) ways you can practice self-care?
Who can be your accountability partner? (It has to be a human.)

As long as this exists,
this sunshine and this
cloudless sky, and as
long as I can enjoy it,
how can I be sad?

—ANNE FRANK,
DIARIST

What are three anxiety-sweat-free events you are looking forward to?

How has a stranger positively affected your life?
What do you wish you could tell them?

Gratitude is a powerful process for shifting your energy and bringing more of what you want into your life. Be grateful for what you already have, and you will attract more good things.

—RHONDA BYRNE, AUTHOR

What act of service makes you feel fulfilled?

Besides "Stop messing with your eyebrows," what advice would you give your teenage self?

I want to thank you
for the profound
joy I've had in the
thought of you.

—ROSIE ALISON,
FILM PRODUCER AND
DIRECTOR

What is the most valuable life lesson you have
learned in the past year? In the past five years?

Joy is a heart full
and a mind purified
by gratitude.

—MARIETTA MCCARTY,
PHILOSOPHER

Which teacher or mentor are you grateful for? Oprah totally counts.

Gratitude doesn't change the scenery. It merely washes clean the glass you look through so you can clearly see the colors.

—RICHELLE E. GOODRICH, POET

What is something difficult you recently did for the first time? How did it make you feel about yourself?

_____

_____

_____

_____

_____

_____

_____

_____

_____

_____

_____

_____

_____

_____

_____

_____

What do you add to other people's lives that they are grateful for?

You have to accept whatever comes, and the only important thing is that you meet it with courage and with the best you have to give.

—ELEANOR ROOSEVELT,
AMERICAN POLITICAL FIGURE
AND FORMER FIRST LADY

What is the hardest or most expensive
professional lesson you have learned?

You just learn
as time passes.

—CARDI B, RAPPER

Make a list of 10 body parts (internal or external) you are most thankful for. Next to each, write a function it serves in your life. Giving them nicknames is optional.

When we give cheerfully
and accept gratefully,
everyone is blessed.

—MAYA ANGELOU, POET

How do you want to be remembered when you're gone?

What does unconditional love look, feel, and sound like?

Look at everything
always as though you
were seeing it either
for the first or last
time: Thus is your
time on Earth filled
with glory.

—BETTY SMITH, AUTHOR

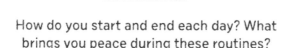

How do you start and end each day? What brings you peace during these routines?

If you had to give up all but five of your physical possessions, what five things would you keep?

I think gratitude is
a big thing. It puts
you in a place where
you're humble.

—ANDRA DAY, MUSICIAN

Who are three ride-or-die humans in your life?

Gratitude brings joy
and laughter into
your life and into
the lives of all
those around you.

—EILEEN CADDY,
TEACHER AND AUTHOR

Snakes on a Plane aside, what three movies
have had the most impact on your life?

Who is a pain in your ass who you love anyway?

If your body could talk, what would it say?
(Besides "Give me tacos.")

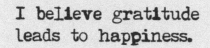

I believe gratitude
leads to happiness.

—NAFESSA WILLIAMS,
ACTOR

What current stressful AF things in your life are you grateful for?

What are your favorite guilty pleasures? You know what?
Screw guilt. Let's just call them regular old pleasures.

Who is your greatest personal loss you're still grieving?
What are you thankful for that they brought into your life?

I still miss those I loved who are no longer with me but I find I am grateful for having loved them. The gratitude has finally conquered the loss.

—RITA MAE BROWN,
ACTIVIST

Who are the people who authentically support you and are genuinely happy for you when you're absolutely crushing it?

Though I am grateful
for the blessings of
wealth, it hasn't changed
who I am. My feet are
still on the ground. I'm
just wearing better shoes.

—OPRAH WINFREY,
AMERICAN MEDIA EXECUTIVE

What is your favorite way to exercise? Yes,
you have to think of at least one.

What separates
privilege from
entitlement is
gratitude.

—BRENE BROWN, RESEARCH
PROFESSOR, AUTHOR,
STORYTELLER

Describe a moment in your life that was
actually really fucking amazing.

What qualities do you deserve in a partner?

Life is not made up of minutes, hours, days, weeks, months, or years, but of moments. You must experience each one before you can appreciate it.

—SARAH BAN BREATHNACH,
AUTHOR

What is your favorite day of the week and how do you like to spend it?

For the yesterdays and todays, and the tomorrows I can hardly wait for— Thank you.

—CECELIA AHERN,
NOVELIST

What are your favorite healthy coping mechanisms?

Write a thank you letter to your body for
the things it helps you accomplish.

If everything
was **perfect, you**
would **never** learn
and you would
never grow.

—BEYONCÉ, SINGER

Who challenges you to be a better version of
yourself without being an asshole about it?

What modern invention that you didn't have
as a child makes your life easier today?

Giving is an expression
of gratitude for our
blessings.

—LAURA ARRILLAGA-ANDREESSEN,
PHILANTHROPIST

How can you show those people in your life who don't suck
(like your friends and family) that you appreciate them?

What are five ways to say "thank you" without words?

A good **life** happens
when you stop and are
grateful **for** the ordinary
moments that so **many**
of us just steamroll
over to try to find those
extraordinary moments.

—BRENE BROWN,
RESEARCH PROFESSOR, AUTHOR,
STORYTELLER

Who was the last person to encourage or praise
you? Did you tell them what it meant to you?

Write down 10 stressful things in your life. Next
to each stressor write what you can do to change
or accept it. Feel free to scream at any time.

The way I see
it, if you want
the rainbow, you
gotta put up
with the rain.

—DOLLY PARTON, SINGER

What qualities do you most admire in others? How do
you acknowledge their positive effect in your life?

What is your favorite season and why is it important
to you? How do you like to spend it?

I am learning every
day to allow the space
between where I am
and where I want to
be to inspire me and
not terrify me.

—TRACEE ELLIS ROSS,
ACTOR AND DIRECTOR

What bougie thing do you like to do to #treatyoself?

Where did you grow up and how did it shape who you are today?

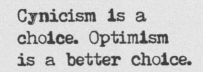

Cynicism is a
choice. Optimism
is a better choice.

—SHONDA RHIMES,
MEDIA PRODUCER
AND WRITER

What risk are you happy you took even though you almost shit yourself while doing it?

Gratitude for the
seemingly insignificant
—a seed—this plants
the giant miracle.

—ANN VOSKAMP,
AUTHOR

What are three activities or hobbies that spark Marie Kondo-level joy in your life? Sleep doesn't count. Well, maybe it does.

Who are three people six feet under —or above—you'd love to thank for having a major influence on your life?

Appreciation can
make a day, even
change a life. Your
willingness to put
it into words is all
that is necessary.

—MARGARET COUSINS,
SUFFRAGIST

What are your favorite (PG) things to do by yourself?

What freedoms are you grateful for? Who helped you earn them?

Gratitude is the closest thing to beauty manifested in an emotion.

—MINDY KALING,
COMEDIAN AND WRITER

When and where do you feel most like yourself?

When was the last time you were vulnerable?
What good came from it?

Gratitude unlocks all
that's blocking us
from really feeling
truthful, really
feeling authentic and
vulnerable and happy.

—GABRIELLE BERNSTEIN,
MOTIVATIONAL SPEAKER

When do you feel most successful? Aside from drinking the
tears of your haters, what does success mean to you?

Which adorable animals have positively affected your life?

Whatever you
appreciate and
give thanks for
will increase in
your life.

—SANAYA ROMAN,
AUTHOR

Who helps make your life less of a nightmare and how can you thank them?

What does gratitude mean to you today? Has that
definition changed since you began this journal?

 GROWING FORWARD

Holy shit—you did it! A moment of silence for the fact that you accomplished filling out this journal when we both know you're busy AF. I'm proud of you. As you reflect back on your time spent with this journal, consider the following:

What are the top three things you have learned about yourself?

1. ....
....
....
....

2. ....
....
....
....

3. ....
....
....
....

What are three favorite prompts you'd like to write more about?

1. ....

....

....

2. ....

....

....

3. ....

....

....

What are the top three things you are most grateful for?

1. ....

....

....

2. ....

....

....

3. ....

....

....

SO YOU'RE A GRATITUDE GENIUS, NOW WHAT?

It's called *practicing* gratitude for a reason. We're never quite done learning how to appreciate all we have in life—which is amazing, because we clearly have an abundance to be thankful for.

As you go forth and prosper, continue to make time for journaling and reflection. You can create your own prompts or simply reflect on your day. Mindfulness, meditation, and journaling are impactful ways to continue your quest. That's right; you're on a fucking quest now. Spread the love, too—consider volunteering at a local nonprofit whose mission you're passionate about or sharing with a friend what you have learned through your writing. Check out the Resources section of this book for more ideas on continuing your gratitude adventure.

I am most thankful for the times
I have been knocked down because,
when I get back up, I turn my
pain into passion. Adversity has
gifted me an abundance of growth,
determination, empathy, and grit.
It has made me who I am today—
and that bitch is amazing.

—TIFFANY REESE,
AUTHOR

RESOURCES

Gratefulness.org A Network for Grateful Living is a global organization offering online and community-based educational programs and practices to inspire and guide a commitment to grateful living, and put into action the life-changing power of personal and societal responsibility.

Headspace.com Headspace has one mission—to improve the health and happiness of the world. Headspace has a free meditation app and website that are valuable resources for both beginners and experts.

Mindful.org Mindful is a mission-driven nonprofit organization dedicated to inspiring, guiding, and connecting anyone who wants to explore mindfulness—to enjoy better health, more caring relationships, and a compassionate society.

PsychologyToday.com *Psychology Today*'s directory provides a comprehensive list of therapists, psychiatrists, and treatment facilities near you. Their website provides resources on gratitude, meditation, mindfulness, and more at no cost.

VolunteerMatch.org VolunteerMatch helps bring together nonprofits and volunteers. VolunteerMatch is a community that believes in the power of volunteering to enrich lives and the world around us.

REFERENCES

Beck, Koa. "20 Quotes from Powerful Women on Gratitude." *Her Money.* March 1, 2019. www.hermoney.com/connect/friends /gratitude-quotes/.

"Brené Brown Quotes About Gratitude." AZ Quotes. Accessed June 13, 2019. www.azquotes.com/author/19318-Brene_Brown /tag/gratitude.

Emmons, Robert. "Why Gratitude Is Good." *Greater Good Magazine.* November 16, 2010. https://greatergood.berkeley.edu/article/item /why_gratitude_is_good.

Haden, Jeff. "40 Inspiring Motivational Quotes About Gratitude." *Inc.* September 12, 2014. www.inc.com/jeff-haden/40-inspiring -motivational-quotes-about-gratitude.html.

Hwang, Haeik, Hyunmi Kang, Jeonghwa Tak, and Sieun Lee. "Impact of Self-Esteem and Gratitude Disposition on Happiness in Pre-Service Early Childhood Teachers." *Procedia–Social and Behavioral Sciences* 174, no. 12. (February 2015): 3447–3453. https://doi.org/10.1016 /j.sbspro.2015.01.1017.

Martinez, Nikki. "73 Gratitude Quotes Celebrating Life, Love & Friends." *EverydayPower* (blog). Accessed June 13, 2019. https://everydaypower.com/gratitude-quotes/.

"Popular Quotes." *Goodreads.* Accessed June 13, 2019. https://www.goodreads.com/quotes.

"7 Perfect Quotes for Thanksgiving from Empowering Women." *Makers* (blog). November 18, 2016. www.makers.com/blog /best-thanksgiving-quotes-gratitude-thankful.

"260 Gratitude Quotes That Will Double Your Happiness." *Wisdom Quotes* (blog). Accessed June 13, 2019. http://wisdomquotes.com /gratitude-quotes/.

Welton, Kathleen. "52 Favorite Gratitude Quotes." Medium. June 12, 2017. https://medium.com/thrive-global/52-favorite-gratitude -quotes-bbf4b09dd57d.

ACKNOWLEDGMENTS

Forever in gratitude to Michael, Jude, Ruby, Ozzy, Bobby, Ari, Alfie, Rufus, Dip Dip, Nini, Papa, Lita, MeMa, the Reeses, Negrons, Smiths, Gollings, Dirties, Doyles, Greeleys, Gordons, Lewises, JBR, AFs, Morgan Shanahan, Callisto Media, Jill Krause, my incredible readers/listeners/Internet besties, Mom2Summit, Zoloft, feminism, dry shampoo, coffee, therapy, music, sugar, *Seinfeld*, expletives, and haters.

ABOUT THE AUTHOR

Tiffany Reese is a writer, podcaster, and body-positive stylist based in Northern California. Tiffany began blogging in 2009, and in 2012 launched LookieBoo.com, a fashion and lifestyle blog focused on children's fashion and creativity. In 2016 Tiffany styled three top-performing BuzzFeed videos focused on body positivity. In 2019 Tiffany wrote, edited, and produced *Something Was Wrong*, an Iris Award–winning podcast about emotional abuse and coercive control.